SERENA WILLIAMS
WINS THE U.S. OPEN

INSTANT REPLAY!

GREAT MOMENTS IN SPORTS, UP CLOSE

BY ELIZABETH NEWMAN

A SPORTS ILLUSTRATED FOR KIDS BOOK

CONTENTS

KERRI STRUG AFTER "THE VAULT"

BRETT HULL ABOUT TO SCORE "THE GOAL"

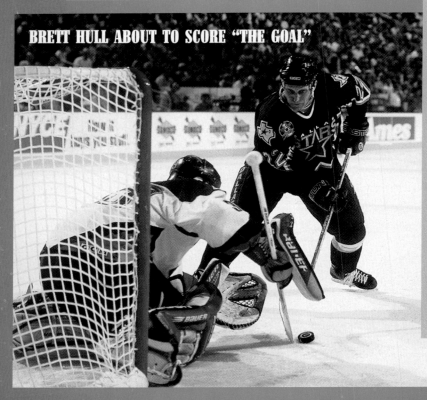

INTRODUCTION 3

Mark McGwire
  THE SWING! 4

Michael Johnson
  THE RACE! 6

Kerri Strug
  THE VAULT! 8

Michael Jordan
  THE LAST SHOT! 10

Lance Armstrong
  THE RIDE! 12

Serena Williams
  THE UPSET! 14

David Cone
  THE PITCH! 16

Maurice Greene
  THE SPRINT! 18

Brett Hull
  THE GOAL! 20

Teresa Weatherspoon
  THE 3-POINTER! 22

John Elway
  THE DIVE! 24

Tony Hawk
  THE TRICK! 26

Briana Scurry
  THE SAVE! 28

Brandi Chastain
  THE KICK! 30

WAY TO GO! 32

INTRODUCTION

WHERE WERE YOU when Mark McGwire slugged his 62nd home run to become baseball's new single-season home-run king? Or when Michael Jordan nailed his last jump shot for the Chicago Bulls to win his sixth NBA championship?

In Instant Replay!, we've pressed the rewind button for you on 14 of the greatest moments in sports. And we've given you the whole picture: a terrific photo of the event, a play-by-play description of what happened, and comments from the athletes about the great moments. Ready, set . . . replay!

3

THE SWING!

MIGHTY MARK McGWIRE BECAME BASEBALL'S NEW HOME-RUN KING

"When Mark first hit the ball, I thought it was a double."
Scott Servais, Cub catcher

"I thought the ball was going to hit the wall. The next thing I know, it disappeared. What an incredible feeling. I did it!"
Mark McGwire, Cardinal batter

"I had the best seat in the house."
Ray Lankford, Cardinal centerfielder

"I was sitting on the edge of the wall. I said, 'That ball is mine!'"
Tim Forneris, grounds-crew worker who found the home-run ball

"I was so excited when Mark hit the ball. I will always remember that moment."
Sammy Sosa, Cub rightfielder

"The pitch was shin-high, off the inside corner. Maybe I will think about giving up the record-breaker after I retire. Right now, it's just another home run. I've given up a billion of them."
Steve Trachsel, Cub pitcher

SEPTEMBER 8, 1998, ST. LOUIS, MISSOURI: St. Louis Cardinal slugger Mark McGwire needed only one home run to break Roger Maris's 37-year-old record of 61 homers in a season. In the fourth inning, Chicago Cub pitcher Steve Trachsel threw Mark a fastball. With one mighty swing of the bat, Big Mac sent the ball sailing 341 feet over the leftfield wall. Number 62! A record for Mark and a new hero for baseball!

"This is storybook stuff. I mean, there can be movies written about things like this. It's like Star Wars and Luke Skywalker. The Force was with Mark McGwire."
Ron Gant, Cardinal leftfielder

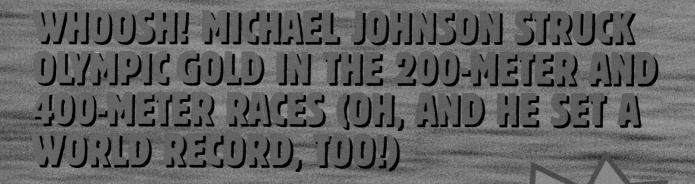

WHOOSH! MICHAEL JOHNSON STRUCK OLYMPIC GOLD IN THE 200-METER AND 400-METER RACES (OH, AND HE SET A WORLD RECORD, TOO!)

"When he passed me, I saw this blue blur. I thought, There goes first."
Ato Bolden, bronze medalist

"I thought when Michael Johnson ran 19.66, it was incredible. For 19.32, I don't know what to say."
Frankie Fredericks, silver medalist

THE RACE!

AUGUST 1, 1996, ATLANTA, GEORGIA: When the gun sounded to start the Olympic 200-meter race, runner Michael Johnson tore out of the blocks. He flew down the track, sailing past his opponents. Just three nights earlier, Michael had won the gold in the 400-meter race. Could he become the first Olympian to win the 200 and the 400? Michael crossed the finish line and glanced at the clock. He hadn't just won the 200, he had set a world record, with a dazzling time of 19.32!

"I've always wanted to bring the two events [the 200-meter and 400-meter races] together in a way that nobody else had ever done. This is the biggest accomplishment of my life."
Michael Johnson

7

THE VAULT!

"She had the willingness and the willpower to make that second jump. She had the courage, the spirit of sacrifice, the toughness."

Bela Karolyi, U.S. women's team coach

TINY KERRI STRUG SHOWED LION-SIZED HEART AS SHE VAULTED THE U.S. TEAM TO GOLD

JULY 23, 1996, ATLANTA, GEORGIA: It was the final event of the U.S. women's gymnastics team competition at the Summer Olympics. All eyes were on tiny Kerri Strug, the last gymnast to vault. Kerri had sprained her ankle on her first vault. It looked as if a good vault from Kerri would wrap up the team gold medal for the U.S.

Kerri sprinted, whirled through the air over the horse . . . and landed solid. As soon as she touched down, she lifted her injured foot in pain. But the deed was done. Kerri scored a 9.712, and the U.S. team won the gold!

"The pain and pressure of one moment were not going to stop me from giving my dream one more run . . . I just said a little prayer and asked God to help me out. I don't know how I did it."
Kerri Strug

"We didn't know if we had won the gold or not. We thought we needed Kerri's second vault. We kept telling Kerri that we couldn't do it without her."
Shannon Miller, U.S. teammate

9

MICHAEL JORDAN ENDED HIS CAREER ON TOP (OF COURSE!) WITH A GAME-WINNER

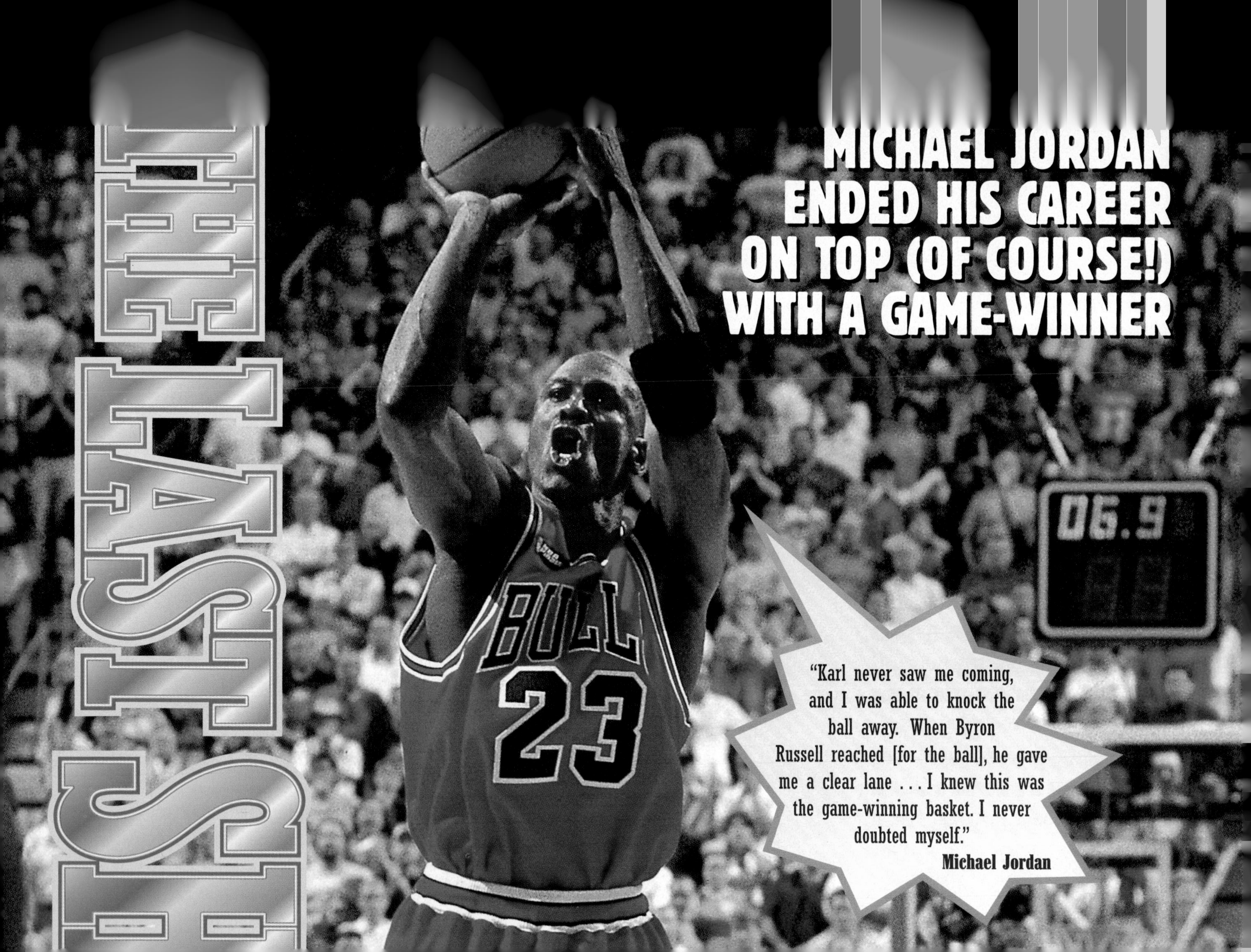

6.90

"Karl never saw me coming, and I was able to knock the ball away. When Byron Russell reached [for the ball], he gave me a clear lane . . . I knew this was the game-winning basket. I never doubted myself."

Michael Jordan

THE LAST SH

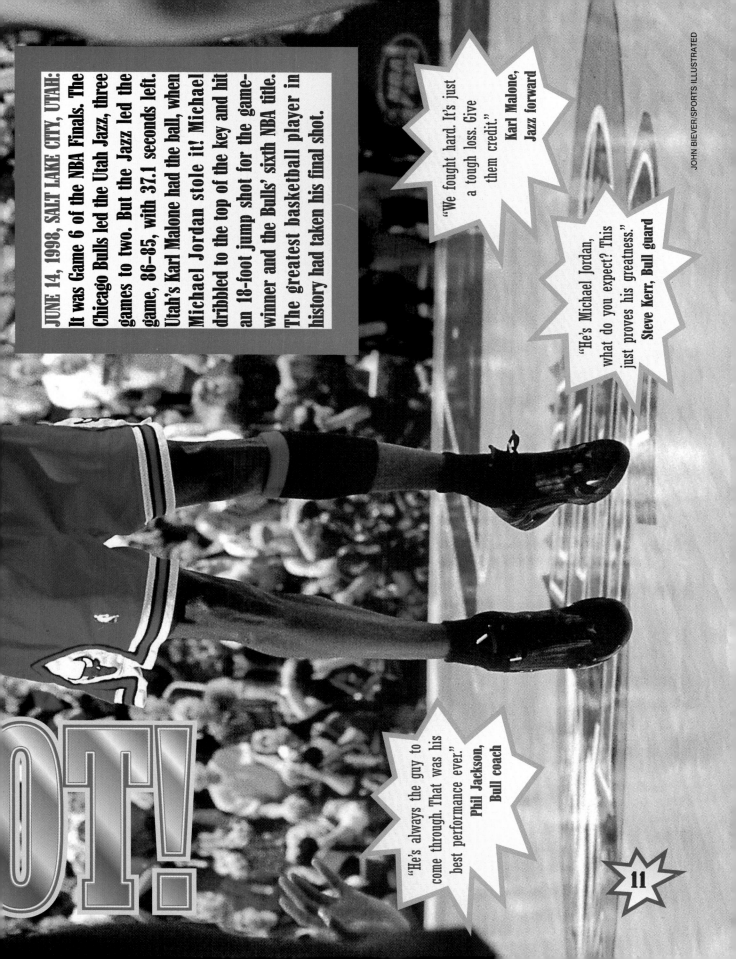

JUNE 14, 1998, SALT LAKE CITY, UTAH: It was Game 6 of the NBA Finals. The Chicago Bulls led the Utah Jazz, three games to two. But the Jazz led the game, 86–85, with 37.1 seconds left. Utah's Karl Malone had the ball, when Michael Jordan stole it! Michael dribbled to the top of the key and hit an 18-foot jump shot for the game-winner and the Bulls' sixth NBA title. The greatest basketball player in history had taken his final shot.

"We fought hard. It's just a tough loss. Give them credit."
Karl Malone, Jazz forward

"He's Michael Jordan, what do you expect? This just proves his greatness."
Steve Kerr, Bull guard

"He's always the guy to come through. That was his best performance ever."
Phil Jackson, Bull coach

OT!

11

THE RIDE!

LANCE ARMSTRONG FOUGHT CANCER, THEN STUNNED THE WORLD WITH HIS WIN IN THE TOUR DE FRANCE

"This is an awesome day. This is beyond belief. If I never had cancer, I never would have won the Tour de France."
Lance Armstrong

"He is a great cyclist, one who is driven by huge motivation and determination."
Alex Zulle, second-place finisher

"In cycling . . . you reach a point where your lungs are on fire and your legs seize up. Most of us are Jeep Cherokees. He's an Indy race car."

Davis Phinney, former U.S. Olympic cyclist and current sportscaster

JULY 25, 1999, FRANCE: When Lance Armstrong crossed the finish line to win the Tour de France, he crowned a comeback that awed sports fans everywhere. Three years earlier, Lance had fought the battle of his life, against cancer. He had undergone treatments, and even brain surgery!

The Tour de France is a grueling, 21-day, 2,287-mile race up and down mountains and through towns in France. Lance finished more than seven minutes ahead of his nearest opponent. He became only the second American to win cycling's premier event.

13

THE UPSET!

"I felt lost out there. I didn't know if Serena was going to hit to my forehand or backhand. I couldn't read her game."
Martina Hingis

SEPTEMBER 11, 1999, FLUSHING, NEW YORK: Was 17-year-old, 7th-ranked Serena Williams about to upset the world's top-ranked woman in the U.S. Open Tennis Championships? Martina Hingis had beaten Serena's older, and more famous, sister Venus the night before in a semi-final match. Would Serena get revenge for the Williams clan now and win the title? After she took the first set, it definitely seemed possible.

The players battled in the second set to force a tiebreaker. At match point, Serena hit a BIG serve. Martina's return went long. Game, set, match, and title to Serena!

SERENA WILLIAMS BEAT THE TOP-RANKED WOMAN IN THE WORLD TO WIN THE U.S. OPEN

"I didn't know if I should laugh, cry, or scream. So I did them all."
Serena Williams

"This is my proudest moment. Words cannot express how I'm feeling."
Richard Williams, Serena's dad

15

THE PITCH!

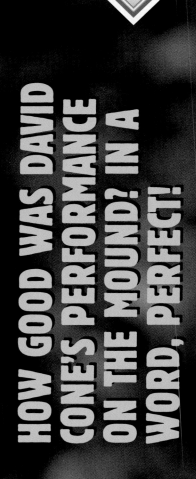

HOW GOOD WAS DAVID CONE'S PERFORMANCE ON THE MOUND? IN A WORD, PERFECT!

"After the fifth inning, I had to fight off thinking about the no-hitter. So in the sixth, I just said, 'Go after them ... You probably have a better chance of winning the lottery than having this happen."
David Cone, Yankee pitcher

"We couldn't find the ball all night. He just threw them straight past me."
Orlando Cabrera, Expo batter

"You think about what he's meant to New York and what he's meant to the Yankees. I don't think it could have happened to a better guy."
Joe Girardi, Yankee catcher

JULY 18, 1999, BRONX, NEW YORK: There were two outs in the top of the ninth inning. New York Yankee pitcher David Cone was one batter away from a perfect game. He threw a sharp slider to Montreal Expo batter Orlando Cabrera. Orlando hit a fly ball into foul territory, and third baseman Scott Brosius made the catch for the final out. David had pitched the 16th perfect game in major league history!

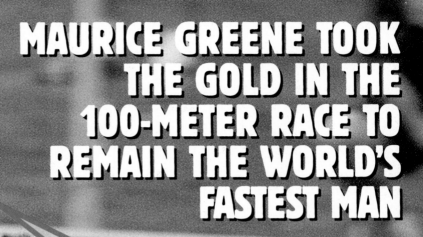

MAURICE GREENE TOOK THE GOLD IN THE 100-METER RACE TO REMAIN THE WORLD'S FASTEST MAN

"I believe if I didn't stumble, that would have been the fastest 100 ever. I didn't panic at all. When I finally started moving, I was just thinking, I can come back and get them. . . . In the end, I was just thinking, I'm glad it's all over!"

Maurice Greene

AUGUST 22, 1999, SEVILLE, SPAIN: Maurice Greene exploded out of the blocks in the 100-meter race at the World Track-and-Field Championships. Then, just as quickly, he stumbled! Would he be able to defend his title? As Maurice stumbled, Bruny Surin of Canada took the lead. The two sprinters ran neck and neck up to the 60-meter mark. Suddenly, Maurice zoomed past Bruny to finish first and win the gold medal!

THE GOAL!

"We won. We are the champions. The Cup is finally mine."

Brett Hull, Star right wing who scored the game-winner

JUNE 19, 1999, DALLAS, TEXAS: Game 6 of the Stanley Cup finals was in triple overtime. At 14:51, Dallas Star right wing Brett Hull shoved the puck past Buffalo Sabre goalie Dominik Hasek for the game-winning and Stanley Cup-winning goal. But wait! Brett's skate was in the crease at the time. A player cannot be in the crease unless he has control of the puck. Did Brett have control? Top official Bryan Lewis said yes and allowed the goal. But many Buffalo fans thought the Sabres got robbed!

"It didn't matter that Hull's skate was in the crease. We determined that Hull played the puck, had possession of the puck, and the goal was good."

Bryan Lewis, director of officiating

20

TERESA WEATHERSPOON'S BUZZER-BEATER WENT SWISH, FROM 52 FEET DOWNTOWN!

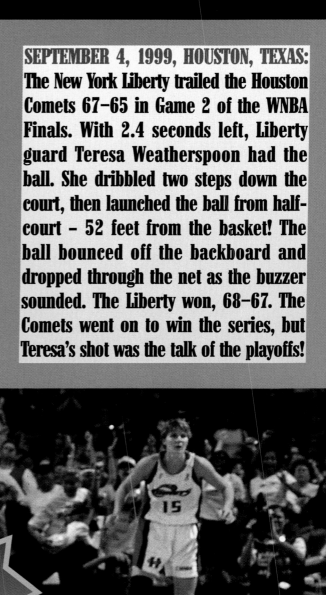

SEPTEMBER 4, 1999, HOUSTON, TEXAS: The New York Liberty trailed the Houston Comets 67–65 in Game 2 of the WNBA Finals. With 2.4 seconds left, Liberty guard Teresa Weatherspoon had the ball. She dribbled two steps down the court, then launched the ball from half-court – 52 feet from the basket! The ball bounced off the backboard and dropped through the net as the buzzer sounded. The Liberty won, 68–67. The Comets went on to win the series, but Teresa's shot was the talk of the playoffs!

"It was just a Hail Mary, and she made it."
Tina Thompson,
Comet forward

THE 3-POINTER!

"When [the ball] left my hands, I knew it was good. I was just praying that it would go in. I've never done this before in a game."
Teresa Weatherspoon

"I thought we were in good shape. I didn't know Teresa would hit a prayer. It's probably the most heart-breaking loss I've ever had."
Van Chancellor, Comet coach

THE DIVE!

"That run, it was like a great made-for-TV movie."
Eugene Robinson,
[former] Packer free safety

"When I saw him do that and then get up pumping his fist, I said, 'It's on.' That's when I was sure we were going to win."
Shannon Sharpe,
Bronco tight end

JANUARY 25, 1998, SAN DIEGO, CALIFORNIA: In Super Bowl XXXII, the Denver Broncos needed a big play. The score was tied, 17–17, in the third quarter. The Broncos had the ball on third down, with six yards to go. Quarterback John Elway dropped back to pass, but no one was open. So John darted downfield, collided with a defensive player, spun into the air, and landed at the four-yard line. First down! The Broncos scored two plays later and went on to win their first Super Bowl in four attempts, beating the Green Bay Packers, 31–24.

JOHN ELWAY CRASH-LANDED FOR THE KEY PLAY AND THE BRONCOS WON THEIR FIRST SUPER BOWL

"When Elway, instead of running out-of-bounds, turned it up and got spun around like a helicopter, it energized us beyond belief."
Mike Lodish, Bronco defensive lineman

"I told myself, 'You've got to do something here. This is what you've been hoping for. Now let's go get this done.' . . . That was the ultimate win. There have been a lot of things that go along with losing three Super Bowls and being labeled as a guy who has never been on a winning Super Bowl team."
John Elway, Bronco quarterback

THE TRICK!

TONY HAWK'S AMAZING 900 HAD FELLOW SKATEBOARDERS AND FANS SAYING "WOW!"

"Tony has been trying the 900 for years. It's monumental to land a trick like that. It won't be done again for years to come."
Andy MacDonald, skateboarder

JUNE 27, 1999, SAN FRANCISCO, CALIFORNIA: No skateboarder had ever mastered the 900, the toughest trick in skateboarding. They either couldn't nail the spins or fell on the landing. But other skateboarders aren't Tony Hawk! With the Summer X Games crowd holding its breath, Tony completed the first 900 in competition history. He turned two-and-a-half rotations high above the halfpipe, landed with a slight touch of the right hand, then rode the trick out clean, to the roar of thousands of fans.

DANA PAUL/ESPN

"This is the best day of my life. This is what it all comes down to. I feel like everything [in my career] has led up to now. That's it for me, I swear. What else is there? The 900 was my goal."
Tony Hawk

"I saw him when he did the kick-flip 540 for the first time. I thought that was great. But this just blows that moment away."
Neal Hendrix, skateboarder

A STOP BY BRIANA SCURRY PUT THE WORLD CUP WITHIN GRASP FOR THE U.S. WOMEN

THE SAVE!

"Bri's [Briana's] save was awesome."
Mia Hamm, U.S. teammate

"I saw Liu's body language when she was walking up to the penalty spot. She didn't look like she really wanted to be there. Her shoulders were slumped, and she looked tired. I thought, 'This is the one.'"
Briana Scurry, U.S. goalie

"That was a great save by Bri. Those are the moments you live for in this sport."
Michelle Akers, U.S. teammate

"After the game I went straight for Bri. I wanted to make sure she knew she was the reason we won the tournament."
Carla Overbeck, U.S. teammate

JULY 10, 1999, PASADENA, CALIFORNIA: The U.S. and China were playing for the Women's World Cup soccer title. After 90 minutes and two overtimes, the score was still 0–0. A shoot-out would determine the winner! Five players from both teams would each take one penalty kick against the opposing goalie. Stopping those kicks would be nearly impossible . . . but key.

With the score of the shoot-out tied at 2–2, Chinese midfielder Liu Yeng drilled the ball toward the net. U.S. goalie Briana Scurry made a spectacular dive to her left and palmed Liu's shot for the save. This could be the edge the U.S. women needed. The Cup was within their reach! (Did they win? Turn the page!)

GOAL! BRANDI CHASTAIN'S GAME-WINNER GAVE THE U.S. WOMEN THE WORLD TITLE

"When I walked up to take the shot, I did not want to make eye contact with Gao because she tends to smile at you and throw you off. When it went in, I thought, 'This is the greatest moment of my life on the soccer field.'"
Brandi Chastain

JULY 10, 1999, PASADENA, CALIFORNIA: The U.S. women's soccer team had one more chance to win the World Cup title in their shoot-out against China. The score of the shoot-out was 4-4, and it was Brandi Chastain's turn to shoot.

With her eyes glued to the ball, Brandi stepped back, then charged forward. With all her might, she kicked a left-footed bullet high into the upper-right corner of the net, past goalkeeper Gao Hong. GOAL!

Brandi's teammates mobbed the field in celebration, and the U.S. women were crowned world champions!

31

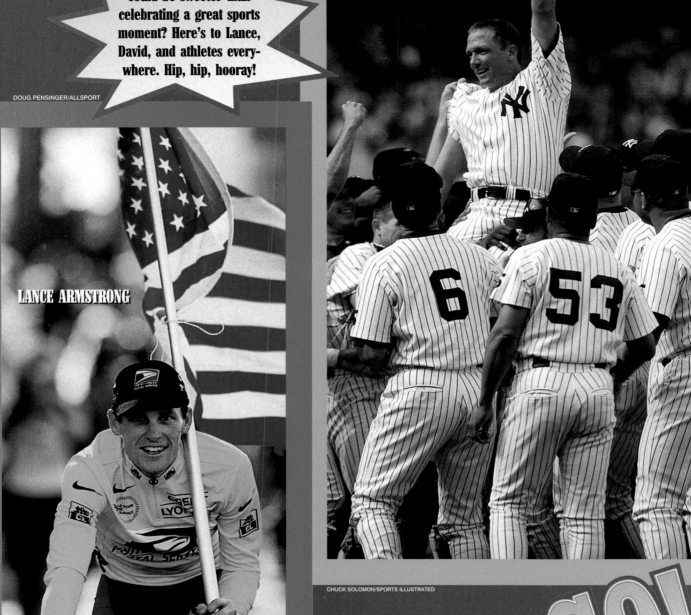

High fives all around! What could be sweeter than celebrating a great sports moment? Here's to Lance, David, and athletes everywhere. Hip, hip, hooray!

DAVID CONE

LANCE ARMSTRONG

WAY TO GO!